Published by Nancy Hall, Inc.
New York, New York 10010

ISBN 1-884270-08-5

10 9 8 7 6 5 4 3 2 1

Printed in Thailand

NURSERY RHYMES

ILLUSTRATED BY ALISON JULIAN

nancy hall, inc.

Jack and Jill

Jack and Jill went up the hill

To fetch a pail of water.

Jack fell down and broke his crown,

And Jill came tumbling after.

Hey Diddle, Diddle

Hey diddle, diddle,

The cat and the fiddle,

The cow jumped over the moon.

The little dog laughed

To see such sport,

And the dish ran away

With the spoon.

Little Miss Muffet

Little Miss Muffet

Sat on a tuffet,

Eating her curds and whey.

There came a big spider,

Who sat down beside her

And frightened Miss Muffet away!

Hickory, Dickory, Dock

Hickory, dickory, dock,

The mouse ran up the clock.

The clock struck one,

The mouse ran down,

Hickory, dickory, dock.

Humpty Dumpty

Humpty Dumpty sat on a wall.

Humpty Dumpty had a great fall.

All the king's horses and all the king's men

Couldn't put Humpty together again.

Jack Be Nimble

Jack be nimble,

Jack be quick,

Jack jump over

The candlestick.

Wee Willie Winkie

Wee Willie Winkie
　　runs through the town,
Upstairs and downstairs
　　in his nightgown,
Rapping at the window,
　　crying through the lock,
"Are the children all in bed,
　　for now it's eight o'clock?"

Star Light, Star Bright

Star light, star bright,

First star I see tonight,

I wish I may, I wish I might,

Have the wish I wish tonight.

Old King Cole

Old King Cole was a merry old soul,

And a merry old soul was he.

He called for his pipe, and he called for his bowl,

And he called for his fiddlers three.

Old Mother Hubbard

Old Mother Hubbard

Went to the cupboard

To fetch her poor dog a bone;

But when she got there,

The cupboard was bare,

And so the poor dog had none.

There Was a Crooked Man

There was a crooked man,

And he walked a crooked mile.

He found a crooked sixpence

Against a crooked stile.

He bought a crooked cat,

Which caught a crooked mouse,

And they all lived together

In a little crooked house.

Jack Sprat

Jack Sprat could eat no fat,

His wife could eat no lean;

And so, between them both, you see,

They licked the platter clean.

Peter, Peter, Pumpkin Eater

Peter, Peter, pumpkin eater,

Had a wife and couldn't keep her.

He put her in a pumpkin shell

And there he kept her very well.

Little Boy Blue

Little Boy Blue, come blow your horn,

The sheep's in the meadow, the cow's in the corn.

Where is the boy who looks after the sheep?

He's under the haystack fast asleep.

Little Bo-peep

Little Bo-peep has lost her sheep

And can't tell where to find them.

Leave them alone, and they'll come home,

Bringing their tails behind them.

This Little Pig

This little pig went to market,

This little pig stayed at home,

This little pig had roast beef,

This little pig had none,

And this little pig cried,

"Wee, wee, wee, wee, wee,"

All the way home.

Little Jack Horner

Little Jack Horner
Sat in a corner,
Eating a Christmas pie.
He put in his thumb
And pulled out a plum,
And said, "What a good boy am I!"

Elsie Marley

Elsie Marley is grown so fine,

She won't get up to feed the swine,

But lies in bed till eight or nine.

Lazy Elsie Marley.

There Was a Little Girl

There was a little girl,
    and she had a little curl
Right in the middle
    of her forehead.
When she was good,
    she was very, very good,
But when she was bad,
    she was horrid.

43

Pussycat, Pussycat

Pussycat, pussycat, where have you been?

I've been to London to look at the Queen.

Pussycat, pussycat, what did you there?

I frightened a little mouse under her chair.